WHALES
Giants of the Deep

STEPHEN LEATHERWOOD

WHALES
Giants of the Deep

DOROTHY HINSHAW
PATENT

<small>Holiday House</small>

<small>NEW YORK</small>

The author would like to express deep apprecia-
tion to Dr. David E. Gaskin, Department of Zool-
ogy, University of Guelph, Ontario, for reading
and evaluating this book.

The photos found on pafes ii, 8, 10, 29, 34, 36, 37, 63, and 64 were
reprinted from Leatherwood, et al. 1982 (S. Leatherwood, R. R.
Reeves, W. F. Perrin and W. E. Evans, 1982. Whales, Dolphins and
Porpoises of the Eastern North Pacific and Adjacent arctic waters. A
Guide to their identification, Washington, D.C. NOAA Technical
Report, NMFS Circular 444. 245 pp.)

Library of Congress Cataloging in Publication Data

Patent, Dorothy Hinshaw.
   Whales, giants of the deep

   Bibliography: p.
   Includes index.
   SUMMARY: An introduction to the largest mammals that ever
lived, with a brief history of whaling and how it has threatened the
whales' survival
      1. Whales—Juvenile literature.   2. Whaling—
Juvenile literature.   [1. Whales.   2. Whaling]   I. Title.
QL737.C4P374 1984   599.5 84-729
ISBN 0-8234-0530-3

Contents

WHALES
Giants of the Deep

The killer whale is a strong, graceful animal,
well adapted to life in the water.
MARINE WORLD/AFRICA USA

1

Giants of the Deep

PEOPLE THINK OF THE EXTINCT DINOSAURS AS HUGE ANI-mals. But there are animals alive today that are even bigger than any known dinosaur—they are whales. Ultrasaurus is the biggest dinosaur yet found. It may have weighed over 100 tons (89 metric tons). But blue whales have been caught that weighed about 120 tons (107 metric tons). Most whales, however, are not that big. Some kinds, like the dwarf sperm whale, get no heavier than 59 tons (51 metric tons).

Although whales live in water and are shaped like fish, they are actually more closely related to dogs and horses. Whales are mammals—warm-blooded animals whose young are born live and feed on milk from the mother's body. Like other mammals, whales breathe air. They cannot get oxygen from the water the way fish can, but must come to the surface for air.

WHALES AND THEIR RELATIVES

The origin of whales is somewhat of a mystery. They seem to have come from the same ancestors as sheep, cows, deer, and giraffes. But those ancestors lived on land, and the first fossil whales already were well adapted for life in water. They had no hind legs, and their front legs were modified into flippers. So far, no fossils of ancestors between four-legged land animals and completely aquatic (water-living) animals with two flippers have been found.

The only close relatives of whales alive today are dolphins

Dolphins look very much like whales, but they are smaller.
NATIONAL PARK SERVICE

and porpoises. Whales, dolphins, and porpoises are quite similar to one another and are very different from any other animals. Their completely aquatic lives require a body plan unlike that of other mammals. The whales, porpoises, and dolphins belong to the scientific order Cetacea (see-TAY-see-ah). The name comes from the Latin word for whale.

The Cetacea are further divided into two different groups. One is called the Odontoceti (Oh-dont-oh-SEE-tee), which means "toothed whales." This group includes the porpoise, dolphin, killer whale, beaked whale, sperm whale, narwhal (NAR-wahl), and beluga (be-LOU-ga) or white whale. The other cetaceans are in the Mysticeti (mi-sti-SEE-tee), which means "mustache whales." These animals have a unique material in their mouths called baleen (bay-LEEN). It is made of closely spaced flexible plates that hang down from the upper jaw, forming a strainer that keeps food in the mouth. We will learn more about baleen later. Baleen whales include the blue, gray, sei (say), fin, right, bowhead, minke (mink), Bryde's (BRU-duhz), and humpback whales.

Sometimes it is not clear whether to call a particular cetacean a porpoise, a dolphin, or a whale. Usually, porpoises have a blunt, rounded snout and dolphins have a more pointed one. The baleen whales are clearly unlike dolphins and porpoises and are always called whales. But some of the smaller toothed whales, such as the pilot whale and the killer whale, may be called dolphins rather than whales.

LIVING IN WATER

All cetaceans share certain traits that make them well suited to their aquatic lives. Most mammals have fur or hair that helps keep their bodies warm, but cetaceans have smooth, hairless skin. Cetacean embryos have some hair, but the only hairs of adults are bristles on the snouts of grays, humpbacks,

Some of the tubercles, or bumps, on the jaws of a humpback whale contain bristly hairs.
GREGORY KAUFMAN, PACIFIC WHALE FOUNDATION

and a few other kinds of whales. In water, hair can slow down swimming. Instead of hair, cetaceans have a thick layer of fat, called blubber, underneath the skin, which insulates them from the cold water. When a cetacean swims, the skin and outer blubber ripple, which helps its body slip smoothly through the water. The blubber of a blue whale can be a foot (30.5 centimeters) thick. The blubber also is a storage site for food.

Most cetaceans have a streamlined shape, with a long head and a short neck. The two halves of the large tail are called flukes. Unlike the fins of fishes, the flukes have no bones in them. The rear third of the body has powerful muscles that

This skeleton of a killer whale shows the handlike bones in the flipper. If you look toward the back, you can also see that there are no hind limbs or tail bones.
GREENPEACE FOUNDATION

are attached to the tail bones of the spine and to the tough fibers of the flukes. Also, unlike the tails of fishes, which move from side to side, the flukes of cetaceans move up and down. During swimming, the upward stroke of the tail powers the animal through the water. The muscles on the top of the spine, which pull the tail upward, are bigger than

The flukes of a cetacean such as those of this killer whale, are powered by very strong muscles.
© PETER THOMAS

You can see small animals called barnacles attached to the tail end and flukes of this gray whale.
BRUCE M. WELLMAN

The flukes of different whales are not shaped the same. You can see how the shape and markings of this blue whale tail fin differ from those of the killer and gray whales.
K. C. BALCOMB/REPRINTED FROM LEATHERWOOD, ET AL. 1982

The humpback whale has long, flexible flippers.
GREGORY KAUFMAN, PACIFIC WHALE FOUNDATION

those on the bottom, which draw the tail down again. The flippers help keep the body stable and are used for steering. Some whales, such as the humpback, have long, especially flexible flippers. A few small bones buried in the muscles are the only remnants of cetacean hind limbs. Many fast-swimming cetaceans have a dorsal fin on the back that helps stabilize the body. Despite their large size, some whales can swim very rapidly. The blue whale is probably the fastest of all cetaceans and can reach speeds of over 30 miles (48 kilometers) per hour. The fin, sei, and killer whales are also speedy swimmers.

The dorsal fin of the humpback is small.
GREGORY KAUFMAN, PACIFIC WHALE FOUNDATION

Cetaceans do not breathe through their mouths. Instead, their nostrils form a special breathing organ on top of the head called a blowhole. It is closed when the animal dives and is opened by special muscles as the animal surfaces. Although most cetaceans have a single blowhole on top of the head above the eyes, the baleen whales have a two-part blowhole. Sperm whales, on the other hand, have a single blowhole on the tip of the snout instead of at the top of the head.

This is the single blowhole of a killer whale.
SEA WORLD PHOTO

Here is the two-part blowhole of a humpback whale.
K. C. BALCOMB/REPRINTED FROM LEATHERWOOD, ET AL. 1982

Cetaceans, especially some whales, can remain underwater for a long time without coming up for air. The sperm whale can stay down for 90 minutes. When whales surface, they let out a visible spout called a blow. The blow of some whales is very distinct. Right whales, for example, have a double, V-shaped blow, while the humpback blow is short and pear-shaped. The blow consists, at least in part, of warm, moist air. The water in the blow condenses into droplets as it hits the atmosphere, making the blow visible. Mucus from the whale's air passages may also make up part of the blow.

A male killer whale blows as he surfaces. © OLIVER THOMAS

The blow of a blue whale can spout very high and looks like a geyser. NOAA

The gray whale blow is low. BRUCE M. WELLMAN

11

Whales have large amounts of a chemical called myoglobin (my-eh-GLOW-bin) in their muscles that carries oxygen. The muscles of other mammals also contain myoglobin, but some whales have eight or nine times as much myoglobin as land mammals do. The muscles of whales are almost black in color from all the dark red myoglobin they contain. When a whale dives, its blood is circulated mainly to the head instead of the body. This way, the oxygen in the lungs goes to the brain, while the myoglobin provides oxygen for the muscles. Once the oxygen is gone, whale muscle can still work and tolerate a lack of oxygen easily.

Cetaceans do not have especially large lungs. But when they breathe, up to 90 percent of the air in the lungs is replaced. Humans only replace 15 percent of the air in their lungs when breathing. This almost complete replacement of the air by whales allows them to carry more oxygen when they dive. After a long dive, a whale pants when it comes to the surface, letting out the stale air in its lungs. The longer the dive, the longer the whale must pant to get rid of the carbon dioxide in its body and to replace the used-up oxygen in its lungs, blood, and muscles.

CETACEAN SENSES

Because cetaceans live in water, they have very different senses from ours. Eyes work well in air, and we rely a great deal on our eyes to tell us about the world around us. But visibility is much lower in water than in air, and light does not penetrate very deeply into the sea. Even at relatively short distances, objects disappear into a blue-green haze. There is almost complete darkness 600 feet (183 meters) beneath the surface, and near the surface, any object more than about 100 feet (30.5 meters) away would be very difficult to see. Be-

This killer whale is spy-hopping. © PETER THOMAS

sides, there are few landmarks in the open ocean that ceta-ceans could use for navigation. The eyes are placed far back on the head in most whales, so they cannot see straight ahead. Some porpoises and dolphins, however, rely on their vision. The bottlenose dolphin has good eyesight, which it uses in catching fast-swimming fish near the surface. Sometimes whales raise their heads straight up out of the water and look sideways toward an object such as a ship on the surface. This is called spy-hopping and is especially noticeable in gray and killer whales.

The sense of smell is well developed in most mammals. Cetaceans, however, have little or no ability to detect odors. Since smell is usually an important part of taste, it may seem surprising that at least some cetaceans appear to have a well-developed sense of taste. Captive dolphins, for example, sometimes have favorite foods.

Cetacean skin is sensitive to touch, and captive dolphins and some whales appear to enjoy being petted by people. Touch probably is also important in their own social life.

The most important sense to these animals is hearing. Water is a much better carrier of sound than air. Sound travels five times as fast in water as in air and may travel much longer distances as well. The ears of whales show on the surface of their bodies only as small holes. They are surrounded by a complicated network of foam-filled sinuses, which help protect the ears from the pressure of great depths. Some scientists believe that these sinuses also isolate the ears from the rest of the head so that the ears are affected only by sound waves traveling directly to them through the water. They

If you look closely, you can see the ear as a small dent just behind the eyes of these leaping bottlenose dolphins.
MARINE WORLD/AFRICA USA

aren't affected by sound passing through the tissues of the rest of the head. But other researchers think that bones or channels of fat in the head help carry sound waves to the ears. The ear canal of the baleen whale is filled by a horny plug, which also may aid in directing sound to the ear bones.

How far sound travels in water depends on its pitch, or frequency. Low-pitched sounds can travel for miles through water, passing right through solid objects. High-pitched sounds don't travel as far, since they bounce off nearby objects.

All whales produce sounds, but whales do not have vocal cords as we do. Toothed whales, dolphins, and porpoises probably use air in the nasal passages to make their high-pitched clicking sounds. These sounds are used to distinguish nearby objects, so in a sense they serve the same function as sight. This use of sound waves to locate objects is called echolocation (ek-oh-lo-CAY-shun), or sonar. It is also used by bats and submarines. A high-pitched sound wave is sent out from the animal. When it hits an object, the wave bounces off and returns in the direction it came from. The animal can tell the location of the object by the time it takes the sound to return. The echo gives information to the signal sender about the distance, direction, and shape of the object from which the signal bounced.

Baleen whales also make sounds of various kinds, and scientists think that all whales use sound to communicate with one another. Bowhead whales make both low- and high-frequency sounds during their migrations, but so far no one has been able to see what the whales are doing when they make the sounds or how other whales respond to them. A little

Like many other cetaceans, the Pacific white-sided dolphin uses sound to communicate with its own kind.
NATIONAL MARINE MAMMAL LABORATORY

more is known about the sound of fin whales. They seem to use high-frequency sounds for communication with other fin whales nearby. Low-frequency sounds are used in long-distance communication. Humpback whales are famous for the "songs" sung by the males. We will learn more about them later.

LONG-DISTANCE TRAVELERS

Whales of one sort or another live in all the world's oceans, and some of them travel great distances during the year. Their travels are necessary to meet their need for food and for reproduction. We think of the tropics as being areas rich in life. That may be true on land, but not at sea. Much of the warm seas near the equator actually harbor little life—certainly not the great quantities of food needed to feed large animals such as whales. The greatest food resources in the oceans are in the northern and Antarctic waters. In order to feed their huge bodies, some whales spend the summer feeding in the north or the Antarctic. Then they travel toward the equator, to protected bays and lagoons, for the winter, when their babies are born.

Life for baby whales is easier in warm waters near the shore. Whereas the adults have thick layers of blubber to insulate them from the cold, young whales have much thinner blubber. Not only that, but because they are smaller than adults, they have a much greater surface area exposed to the water for their size (see page 23). For both these reasons, young whales lose heat from their bodies more easily than adults do.

Gray whales have the longest migration of any mammal. They travel up and down the Pacific coast of North America, making a round trip of about 10,000 miles (16,000 kilometers) each year. During the summer, they feed in the rich Arctic waters of the Bering Sea. In the fall, they swim down the coast to the warm, protected lagoons of Baja California, Mexico. There they bear their young and mate once again. Humpback whales in the Pacific travel from the bays of the Hawaiian Islands and Mexico, where they spend the winter, to Alaskan waters, where they feed in the summer.

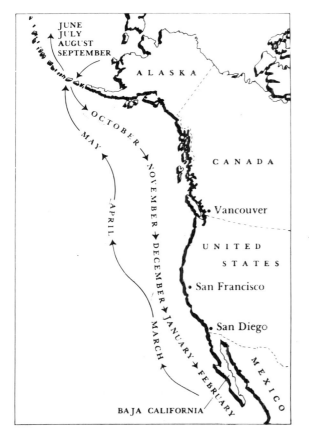

The gray whale migrates from the icy Bering and Chukchi seas in the high western Arctic to the warm lagoons of Baja California, Mexico. MAP © 1980 BY RICHARD ELLIS. USED BY PERMISSION.

During their time in warm waters, many kinds of whales do not feed. They use up the energy stored in the thick blubber layers they've built up while feeding in northern or Arctic waters. Because the water is warm, the whales don't need as much insulation from the environment, so losing the blubber doesn't make life more difficult for them.

BEARING YOUNG

Whales have only one baby at a time, rarely twins. After birth, the mother takes good care of her baby. She stays with it and protects it from danger. Whalers used to take advantage of the protectiveness of the mother whale. They would harpoon a baby and then attack the mother when she came to the aid of her young one.

Cetacean mothers, like this female captive killer whale, stay close to their young and protect them from danger.
MARINELAND, RANCHO PALOS VERDES, CA

The young whale feeds on milk produced by the mother's body. The nipples from which the baby gets the milk protrude from a groove in the mother's belly. When the baby isn't nursing, the groove is closed, keeping the mother's body streamlined. Because it needs to breathe, a baby whale can't nurse for very long at a time. It must often come up for air. The baby's feeding is speeded up, however, because muscles in the mother's milk-producing glands contract and squirt the milk into the young whale's mouth.

After mating, female baleen whales carry the growing young whale for 10 to 12 months before it is born. Toothed whales, on the other hand, probably bear their young over a year after mating. Mother whales sometimes nudge their babies to the surface for their first breath. After it is born, the mother nurses her calf for 5 to 7 months. Humpback mothers, however, nurse for 10 months or even more, and Greenland right whales nurse for perhaps a year. Sperm whales, on the other hand, carry the developing baby for 16 months and feed it for about 2 years. Most whales probably have calves every 2 years. Sperm whales, however, give birth only every 3 years, and humpbacks may sometimes give birth once a year.

THE SIZES OF WHALES

Even the smallest whales are big by human standards. The dwarf sperm whale, at 8½ feet (2.6 meters) in length, is much longer than a man is tall. Several of the smaller whales range from 15 to 20 feet (4.6 to 6 meters) long. But the most impressive of all are the "great whales." These are the giants of the sea that were brutally hunted down by whalers for their valuable meat, blubber, baleen (in some), and other natural products. The "great whales" include all of the baleen whales, except for the pygmy right whale, and two of the toothed whales—the sperm and killer.

Among the baleen whales, the females are usually larger than the males. For example, an average-sized female blue whale is about 81 feet (25 meters) long, while a male is around 76 feet (23 meters). Among toothed whales, however, the males are the true giants. A male sperm whale can be twice as long as a female. Males as long as 50 feet (15 meters) are common, with some up to 60 feet (18.2 meters). Female sperm whales are usually no longer than 38 feet (11.5 meters).

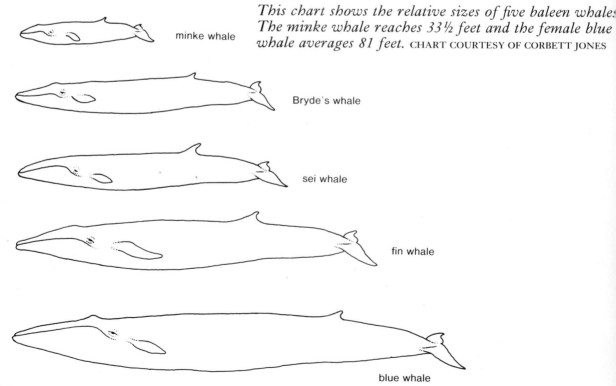

This chart shows the relative sizes of five baleen whales. The minke whale reaches 33½ feet and the female blue whale averages 81 feet. CHART COURTESY OF CORBETT JONES

minke whale

Bryde's whale

sei whale

fin whale

blue whale

GROWING FAST

How do whales get so big? The fertilized egg of a whale is the same size as that of other mammals, smaller than a pinhead. But while it is inside its mother's body, the baby whale grows extremely fast. During the first weeks of development, the whale embryo grows slowly and looks like that of other mammals. It even develops the tiny buds that in other mammals become the hind legs. But when the embryo is about 1 inch long, it begins to look like a whale, and the hind-limb buds disappear. After three months, a blue whale embryo is about a foot long. Its flippers have formed, and its tail flukes are present. It is unmistakably a developing cetacean. From then on, the embryo increases rapidly in size, putting on most of its bulk during the final 3 months before birth. When born, after 11 months of development, the baby blue whale is 25 feet (7.6 meters) long and weighs 2 tons (1.75 metric tons).

After being born, a young whale continues its spectacular growth rate—a week-old blue has already doubled its birth weight! This means that it gains almost 24 pounds (11 kilograms) an hour. By comparison, it takes a human baby 120 days to double its far more modest weight at birth. The young whale grows with the help of its mother's rich milk. A large female whale produces over 130 gallons (500 liters) of milk every day, all of which her baby drinks. The milk is not only plentiful but very rich—it contains as much as 50 percent fat (cow's milk averages only 4 percent fat). By the time a young blue whale is weaned from its mother and no longer drinks her milk, it is already a true giant at about 50 feet (15.2 meters) long.

Toothed whales, like this baby killer, are born tail first.
At least some baleen whales, however, are born headfirst.
MARINELAND, RANCHO PALOS VERDES, CA

WHY SO LARGE?

What advantages are there for whales in being so large? Why are they so much bigger than anything that lives on land? Several factors are involved in the giant size of whales. An important principle dealing with size is the surface-to-volume ratio. As an object increases in size, its volume increases much faster than its surface area. For example, compare a one-inch or one-centimeter cube with a two-inch or two-centimeter cube. The first cube has a volume of 1 cubic inch (1 centimeter) and a surface area of 6 square inches (6 square centimeters). Its surface area is six times its volume. The second cube, however, has a volume of 8 cubic inches (8 cubic centimeters) and a surface area of 24 square inches (24 cubic centimeters), only three times as much as the volume. The larger an object is, the less surface area it has compared with its volume. Because of the surface-to-volume ratio, big land animals like elephants can have problems staying cool. A mammal's body produces heat in order to keep the body temperature stable. If the air is cool, the heat produced will keep the body warm. But if the outside temperature is hot, a mammal needs a way to keep from overheating. A big animal, such as an elephant, has a limited surface area from which it can release extra heat. It cools itself by flapping its big ears and heading for water, using its trunk to douse itself. Also, because they are so heavy, elephants, like other big land animals, must have thick bones and wide legs to support their weighty bodies and carry them around. Land animals can't get too large, or they wouldn't be able to move about.

A whale, on the other hand, doesn't have to support its body. The water supports it, so size in itself is no disadvantage. As a matter of fact, there are definite advantages to

being big. For one thing, larger animals have fewer enemies than smaller ones. The only enemies of whales, other than humans, are big sharks and other whales. Killer whales, for example, will sometimes attack whales of other kinds. In the sea, the water temperature is quite constant in one area and is cooler than the body temperatures maintained by whales, about 100 degrees Fahrenheit (37.8 °c). Cooling off is rarely a problem, but keeping warm can be. Because of its large surface area, a small cetacean must eat great quantities of food in order to produce the heat to keep its body warm. For example, a harbor porpoise consumes about ten percent of its body weight in food a day. But because of its relatively smaller surface area, a great whale can eat less for its size and yet manage to stay warm. It can eat five percent of its weight daily and put on blubber in the process. This is still an enormous amount of food—a blue whale may consume 4 tons (3.6 metric tons) of food in one day!

WHALE DWELLERS

Whales are like moving islands in the sea. Their bodies provide homes for several kinds of other animals. Large barnacles attach themselves to some kinds of whales. So many barnacles infest the heads of gray whales at times that they form solid white areas. All adult humpbacks carry large barnacles, sometimes 3 inches (7.5 centimeters) in diameter. Other barnacles burrow right into the whale's skin. These barnacles do not depend on their host for food, for they feed on tiny animals adrift in the sea.

The killer whale isn't all that big by whale standards, but it is huge compared to a human being.
MARINE WORLD/AFRICA USA

Small animals sometimes bother whales, but they aren't a major threat. On the snout of this humpback whale, you can see scars from barnacles which once were attached to it, as well as a white scar on the upper jaw, to the left of the person, which was made by a cookie-cutter shark.
GREGORY KAUFMAN, PACIFIC WHALE FOUNDATION

Unlike barnacles, whale lice do feed on whale skin. They are especially common on gray, humpback, and right whales. Whale lice are flat crustaceans (relatives of shrimp and crabs) with strong claws that allow them to cling tightly to the whales. They live in skin folds, among the knobs of humpbacks, and on the head calluses of right whales.

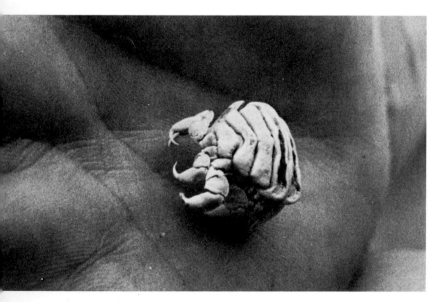

You can see the sharp, strong claws the whale louse uses to hang onto its host.
DOUGLAS MACPHAIL,
C/O PETER THOMAS

2

Baleen Whales

MOST OF THE GREAT WHALES THAT HAVE BEEN HUNTED BY whalers have baleen. There are only ten or eleven kinds, or species, of baleen whales. The greatest number are very large animals. Only the pygmy right whale is "small"—it rarely grows longer than 20 feet (6 meters). The blue whale, the largest animal of all, can reach 100 feet (30.5 meters) in length.

The baleen whale is found in almost all the world's oceans. It has a blowhole with paired openings. Each opening corresponds to a nostril. A ridge runs along the top of the head, from the tip of the snout to the blowhole. It spreads out at the blowhole, surrounding the two holes so that they are elevated a bit above the top of the head.

A humpback surfaces, revealing its blowhole with paired openings. GREGORY KAUFMAN, PACIFIC WHALE FOUNDATION

As mentioned earlier, baleen whales have no teeth. Instead, they have rows of baleen plates that rim the upper jaws. The plates are made of the same material as hair and fingernails and hang down around the edges of the mouth. They are about one-quarter inch (0.63 centimeters) thick and are spaced about one-quarter inch apart. There are as many as 450 plates on each side in the fin whale's mouth. Each baleen plate is shaped like a triangle. One side is anchored to the upper jaw. The baleen varies greatly in size, depending on the species, but the longest plates are always in the middle area of the jaw. The baleen of the right whale is long and narrow. It is less than a foot (30.5 centimeters) wide at the base but can be 7 feet (about 2 meters) long. Blue whales, however, have short, wide baleen that is almost 2½ feet (75 centimeters) wide and no more than 2 feet (60 centimeters)

This is the baleen from the right side of a fin whale, lying upside down on the dock. You can see some of the frayed inner material which helps strain out food along the bottom of the baleen. Notice that the front third of the baleen is white, while the back part is black. The baleen on the left side is not white in front. NOAA

long. The outer edges of the baleen are smooth. But the inner edges look frayed, with fibers that form a filtering mat. When the baleen whale feeds, it gathers food into its mouth. Then it closes its mouth partially and forces water out between the baleen plates. The fibers of the baleen act like a sieve, holding back the food in the mouth. Then the food is swallowed.

In this close-up, you can clearly see the individual baleen plates with their frayed edges.
T. HOBAN/REPRINTED FROM LEATHERWOOD ET AL. 1982

A side view of one baleen plate. Note the triangular shape and the frayed inner edges.
COURTESY OF CORBETT JONES

Right Whales

There are three kinds of right whales—the Greenland right whale, also called the bowhead; the black right whale; and the pygmy right whale. The black right whales are sometimes divided into two species, southern and northern.

This close-up of a right whale shows its long, semi-circular blowholes. J. E. SCARFF

Little is known about the pygmy right whale, which lives only in the southern oceans and either is very rare or spends a great deal of time underwater, where people can't see it. The bowhead and the black right whale are better known. Both can be up to 60 feet (18.2 meters) long, are black, and have huge heads with very long baleen. Some right whales have white on their belly. The top jaw bones curve upward in the middle, making room for the long baleen, which is covered when the mouth is closed by the huge, arched lower lip.

This unusual lower lip gives these whales a uniquely curved mouth. The bowhead lives only in the Arctic Ocean, while the black right whale lives in all the oceans.

The right whale got its name from the old-time whalers, who considered these giants the "right" whales to kill, since their thick blubber yielded valuable oil and their long baleen had a variety of uses. Right whales were easy to attack, since they swim slowly and often come into shallow waters to breed and raise their young. Because it has so much blubber, the right whale carcass floats easily, too, which was important to whalers.

The black right whale was once very plentiful throughout the world's seas, but now, because it was hunted so mercilessly, it is among the rarest of whales. The black right whale is easy to identify because it lacks a dorsal fin and has strange, hardened growths on its head. The growths are several inches thick, and their exact arrangement is unique to each individual whale. No one knows the function of these lumps and bumps.

The bowhead has the biggest head and the longest baleen of all the baleen whales. The head takes up as much as one-third of the body's length. The huge mouth with its bowed outline can be 8 feet (2.5 meters) wide and 16 feet (5 meters) long, and the gigantic tongue can weigh a ton. Bowhead baleen over 15 feet (4.6 meters) long has been measured. One bowhead may carry a ton of baleen in its mouth; laid end

A bowhead whale. COURTESY OF CORBETT JONES

to end, the baleen would cover the length of a mile (1.6 kilometers). With its chunky black body, peculiar head, and white chin, the bowhead is easy to recognize.

While many whales migrate from north to south, the bowhead spends its entire life in Arctic waters, moving from one area to another with the seasons. Bowheads are now so rare that it is difficult to track their migrations, but they move over considerable distances through northern waters.

The Eskimos, or Inuit, have hunted bowheads for close to four thousand years. The whales arrive near Inuit shores in the springtime, when a joyful festival welcoming whales and the warmer time of year is held. The men hunt the whales, and the villagers share in the bounty provided by successful hunters. The bowhead is an important part of coastal Inuit life. Yet it is the most endangered of all the great whales. Although it was white whalers who brought the bowhead to the verge of extinction, it is the Inuit who now are placed in a difficult position. Some scientists believe that any hunting at all will spell final doom for the bowhead. But the Inuit believe that if they are not allowed to carry out their annual whale hunt, their culture is doomed. Since 1935, only the Inuit have been allowed to hunt the bowhead.

Eskimos at Barrow, Alaska, celebrate a successful bowhead hunt with a feast called the Nalukatak, or Blanket Toss. Singing, dancing, and the eating of whale skin, blubber, and other traditional foods are also part of the event. THE ARCTIC POLICY REVIEW

THE SPEEDY RORQUALS

While the right whales are stout-looking and slow, many other baleen whales are slim, streamlined, and fast. These are the rorquals (ROAR-kwelz), which include the fin, sei, minke, Bryde's, and blue whales. The word *rorqual* comes from the Norwegian word for furrow. A series of grooves runs along the underside of the rorqual's body, from the edge of the jaw to as far back as the navel. The grooves allow the mouth to expand during feeding. The rorqual's body is long and graceful, with a triangular dorsal fin placed far back. A ridge runs from front to back along the top of the head. The rorquals are not only the largest of animals, they are among the fastest in the sea. The baleen of rorquals is short. All rorquals seem to migrate, but just where some of them go when not feeding in polar seas is not known.

The blue whale is the largest animal in the world. In this photo, you can see the grooves which run from the front of its head all the way to its navel. NOAA

33

Minke whales which live in the north have a white band on each flipper, as you can see in this photograph.
D. CALKINS/REPRINTED FROM LEATHERWOOD, ET AL. 1982

You can see the single ridge along the top of this sei whale's head. The dappled design is from the water and is not part of the whale's coloration.
GORDON WILLIAMSON, COURTESY OF GENERAL WHALE/REPRINTED FROM LEATHERWOOD, ET AL. 1982

The minke whale is the smallest rorqual, reaching 33½ feet (10.2 meters) long. Its body is dark gray to black above and white underneath, and it has a pointed snout. Most northern minke whales have a white patch on each flipper. A ridge runs along the top of the whale's head. Minke whales usually travel alone or in groups of two to four. They are the only species still hunted in large numbers.

The sei whale was named for the Norwegian word for a fish we call the pollack, because both show up off the Norwegian coast at the same time of year. It is dark gray-blue color, with white markings below. Sei whales can reach 65 feet (19.8 meters) in length.

Little is known about Bryde's whale. It looks much like the sei and fin whales, except that it has three ridges along the top of its head instead of the usual one. Only in 1913 did scientists realize that Bryde's whale was a separate species from the sei whale. Even after that, whalers often did not distinguish between the two kinds. Bryde's whale doesn't migrate long distances, tending instead to stay in the tropics.

The fin whale, named for its tall dorsal fin, is the second largest whale and may be as long as 82 feet (25 meters). Most fin whales, especially in the north, are quite a bit smaller than this. Although a large fin whale may weigh 50 tons (45 metric tons), it is lighter than a blue whale of the same length, because it is slimmer. The fin whale can swim rapidly for long periods of time, averaging up to 9 miles (14.5 kilometers) per hour, and can swim as fast as 20 miles (32 kilometers) per hour in short bursts. This graceful and speedy whale has been called the "greyhound of the sea." The coloration of the fin whale is unique. The lower jaw is black on the left side and white on the right. The baleen is also differently colored on the two sides. This unusual color pattern is not completely understood, although it is probably related to the fin whale's habit of turning on its side when it feeds.

The magnificent blue whale is the largest of all. Despite its size, it is a graceful animal. Its color is a grayish blue that looks quite blue when seen in the water. This whale also has scattered light spots, mostly on the back and shoulders. The underside is the same color as the back.

You can see the light color on the right side of the head of this fin whale.
H. E. WINN/REPRINTED FROM LEATHERWOOD, ET AL. 1982

THE HUMPBACK

Humpbacks are medium-sized whales, reaching 50 feet (15 meters) in length. The humpback is closely related to the rorquals, but its body is more stout and not so streamlined. Like the rorquals, humpbacks have grooves running from the chin to the belly that allow the mouth to expand during feeding. Humpbacks, however, average twenty-eight grooves, while a blue whale can have over ninety. The dorsal

This humpback is settling back into the water upside down after jumping from the water (breaching). You can see barnacles on its flipper and snout as well as the grooves on the underside.
K. C. BALCOMB/REPRINTED FROM LEATHERWOOD, ET AL. 1982

fin is variable in shape and size. Scattered on the head, the humpback has knobby bumps or tubercles, each about the size of a fist, which contain bristles. Its flippers are huge, the largest of any whale's, reaching to a length of 15 feet (4.6 meters). The basic humpback color is black on top and white below, but there is much variation. Some humpbacks are almost completely black, while others have white reaching up around the sides.

At the turn of the twentieth century, about twelve thousand or more humpback whales wandered through the North Pacific. Today, fewer than one thousand exist, because of the relentless hunting that went on until 1966. Fortunately, humpbacks also live in other areas of the world. They breed along both coasts of South America and Africa and on the west and east coasts of Australia as well as near various Pacific islands. Southern humpbacks migrate to the Antarctic to feed, while northern ones travel as far north as Greenland and the Bering Sea.

In some ways we know more about this species than any of the other baleen whales. There are several reasons for this. For one, many humpbacks come to the quiet lagoons of the Hawaiian Islands, where scientists study them, to bear their young and to breed each winter. Humpbacks are difficult to investigate since they spend only about 10 percent of their time at the surface. On the other hand, they are not afraid of humans. So as long as scientists are willing to join them in their underwater homes, humpbacks can be easily observed.

Individual humpbacks can be told apart with no difficulty. The dorsal fins are very different in shape and the proportions of black and white vary from whale to whale. Even more distinctive is the exact pattern of black and white on the underside of the tail flukes, which can identify individual

*As the humpback dives, you can see the humped appearance
of its back which gives it its name.*
GREGORY KAUFMAN, PACIFIC WHALE FOUNDATION

The humpback has knobby tubercles on its head.
GREGORY KAUFMAN, PACIFIC WHALE FOUNDATION

whales just as fingerprints identify individual people. Scientists have taken photographs of the flukes of hundreds of humpbacks in different locations in both the Atlantic and Pacific Oceans, allowing them to identify the same whale in different places. This way, individual whales can be traced and their activities followed.

A fascinating humpback activity is its famous "singing." While many whales make sounds of various sorts, no other whale appears to have a song like the humpback's. Humpbacks only sing while in their southern breeding grounds, and so far, all singers have been identified as males. The singer hangs in the water, head down, within 150 feet of the surface, at about a 45 degree angle. The flippers are stretched out. The songs last from 6 to 30 minutes and consist of from two to eight different themes. Once a whale is finished with the song, it may repeat it after only a brief pause. Humpbacks have been known to continue singing, repeating the same song over and over, for as long as 24 hours. This whale music is eerie and strange but somehow quite beautiful. It is loud enough for a human to hear over a mile away underwater. All the humpbacks in the same area sing an identical song, and the songs change over time. After a few years, the song used in a particular place has changed completely from what it used to be.

Because all the male humpbacks in one area sing the same song, which is different from that of whales in other places, the movements of humpback populations can be followed by recording the songs. Humpbacks can also be traced because of the differences in their flukes. Using these methods, researchers have found that individual humpbacks may wander great distances and not always follow the same migration path. It was once thought that the humpbacks that winter in

Hawaii spent the summer feeding near the Aleutian Islands in the far western part of Alaska. Humpbacks that spend the winter near Baja California, Mexico, which is just south of the state of California, were believed to spend the winter near southern Alaska, far east of where the Hawaiian humpbacks went. People believed that these two groups of whales always remained separate. But the songs of the Baja California humpbacks are the same as the Hawaiian ones, and two humpbacks identified by their flukes were found in both places. Seven Hawaiian humpbacks were found summering in southeastern Alaska, too. It seems, then, that humpbacks move about a great deal, roaming over thousands of miles of ocean. An individual may spend one winter in Hawaii and another winter near Baja California.

Scientists have also studied how humpback mothers raise their young. The mother often has help with her baby in the form of an "escort" whale. Once, escorts were thought to be other females that hadn't had babies of their own. But every escort identified so far has been a male, probably one waiting for his chance to mate with the female. The baby whale needs to surface for air every few minutes while it is young, and the mother goes with it. The escort remains below, surfacing by itself when it needs oxygen. With two adults to protect it, the baby humpback has a good chance of survival.

While the baby whales are feeding and gaining over 50 pounds (22 kilograms) a day, the adult whales apparently do not feed at all. They gorge themselves at the northern feeding grounds during the summer, putting on tons of blubber, which nourishes them for the 4 to 6 months of fasting. As the mother's blubber becomes thinner, the baby puts on a good layer of its own to protect it from the colder Alaskan seas when the humpbacks again travel northward for the summer.

THE GRAY WHALE

The gray whale is unique among baleen whales. Instead of a dorsal fin, the gray has a row of bumps along its back, starting about where a dorsal fin might be and extending all the way to the tail. Female gray whales can reach 50 feet (15 meters), and are generally larger than the males. Because they migrate up and down the west coast of North America, where they can easily be watched, gray whales are familiar to many people. From June through September they feed in northern waters. Then they begin their long migration southward. The whales travel singly or in small groups. They swim steadily onward, for about 20 hours a day, covering 60 to 70 miles (100 to 110 kilometers) a day. By the time they have reached Baja California, three months have gone by and they have traveled 5,000 miles (8,000 kilometers). The pregnant females reach the protected wintering grounds

The snout of the gray whale is often covered with barnacles.
BRUCE M. WELLMAN

42

You can see the patchy gray coloration of the gray whale in this photo. BRUCE M. WELLMAN

first and soon give birth. The adult males and young whales arrive later. The whales remain in the warm lagoons, the females and young in deep water, the males stationed near the entrances, for 2 or 3 months. Then they return northward, back to their feeding grounds. It is possible that some gray whales feed during the migration, but probably they do not. The blubber they build up during their 4 months of northern gorging is enough to nourish them for the rest of the year.

The gray whale disappeared from the Atlantic Ocean a long time ago, and another population near the Korean coast is either gone or very small. But the Pacific gray whale provides the only success story so far for whales recovering from the horrors of whaling. Gray whales were killed by the thousands during the late 1800s, until there were too few for whalers to bother with. Then, during a surge of whaling in the 1920s, most of the few remaining grays were taken. By the time it was completely protected in 1938, the gray whale population had dwindled to only a few dozen, and conservationists feared that this magnificent animal would die out. The gray whale, however, made an amazingly rapid and successful comeback. By the 1960s, there were about eleven thousand of them living along the Pacific coast of North America, and that number has remained stable since. If we could understand the reasons for this success, perhaps we could provide better conditions for the recovery of the other species of great whales.

FEEDING HABITS

It may seem strange that the biggest animals, baleen whales, feed on some of the smallest animals, various shrimplike creatures that live in the ocean. But actually it makes sense, for those small animals feed on the most plentiful living things in the sea, so they themselves are extremely numerous.

The surface waters of the ocean can be swarming with life. Tiny single-celled green plants called algae drift along the surface, using the energy of the sun to manufacture food and to multiply. Small animals float along with the algae, feeding on them and on one another. This mixture of floating life is called plankton. Many tiny, shrimplike animals live in the plankton in very large numbers. These are the major food of baleen whales, along with small, schooling fish.

Baleen whales have different methods of catching their food. Right whales swim through patches of plankton near the surface with their mouths open. Often, the front part of the upper jaw is raised up out of the water. Water containing plankton enters the mouth. The water exits through the gaps in the baleen as the animal swims, but the tangled mat of fibers on the inner edges of the baleen keeps the food from leaving. When enough plankton has accumulated, the whale swallows. The right whale's baleen plates are very close together. The long, flexible baleen collapses together and lies pointing backward when the mouth is closed. When the mouth opens, the baleen springs downward again, ready to act as an effective sieve. The large lower lip holds the tips of the baleen in place while the whale feeds. The right whale's way of feeding is called skimming.

The faster-swimming rorquals feed in a different way. Instead of gradually filling up the mouth with food, they take in great gulps of water, then strain out the plankton by squeezing the water through the baleen. Again, the hairy edges of the baleen keeps the food from leaving with the water.

The blue whale seems to be the champion "gulper." It swims up to the food, opens its huge mouth, then closes it, engulfing 70 tons of water at once. When full of water, the mouth is greatly expanded, with the pleated grooves along the throat ballooned out to make room for the water and food. After closing its mouth and entrapping the plankton, the blue whale opens its lips and squeezes the water out through the gaps between the baleen plates.

The fin and sei whales feed in a similar fashion, but their throats do not become as remarkably expanded as that of the blue whale. Also, sei whales are gulpers when they feed on fish, but resort to skimming while eating plankton.

As mentioned earlier, many blue, sei, and fin whales migrate to the Antarctic to feed during our winter months, when it is summer down south. Among the most abundant of all the animals in their southern diet are the shrimplike crea-

This photo of a blue whale feeding was taken from the air. The whale is on its side, and you can see the enormously enlarged throat clearly. RONN STORRO-PATTERSON

tures called krill. Krill are only an inch or two long, but they occur in gigantic masses in the Antarctic Ocean. A swarm of krill can cover the area of several city blocks and may be over 15 feet (4.4 meters) deep. A cubic yard of such a group may contain 63,000 individuals! Krill are the chief food of baleen whales that migrate to the Antarctic to feed. Other blue, fin, and sei whales feed in the north, where they consume different, small shrimplike animals.

There are variations in the feeding of baleen whales beyond skimming and gulping. For example, gray whales feed on small bottom-dwelling animals by sucking up mouthfuls of mud and then straining out the food organisms with the baleen. The head of the gray whale, especially along the right side, is usually covered with scars and scrapes, which result from scraping along the bottom. Apparently, however, the grays feed little or not at all during their migrations, which was when they were hunted. Since captured gray whales rarely had any food in their stomachs, it was difficult to tell what these giants ate.

This close-up of a blue whale's underside while feeding shows the expanded pleats clearly. RONN STORRO-PATTERSON

Humpbacks have a variety of unique ways of feeding. They often feed on shrimp or schooling fish, which can move faster than krill and other plankton. Humpbacks "corral" their prey, using screens or clouds of bubbles that they create under the water, apparently by letting air out of the blowhole. The whale comes up inside the circle of bubbles with its mouth open, engulfing the water and shrimp or fish inside the bubbles. Sometimes, several humpbacks will feed together. Groups of whales may create bubble clouds in the same area, then feed together among the bubbles. Or, five or six whales may feed side by side without the aid of bubbles. Instead, they go underwater and rise together, mouths open, toward the surface. Individual humpbacks also feed by lunging upward from beneath the surface with their mouths open. As much as a third of the body emerges from beneath the surface during this lunge feeding. When humpbacks eat, the throat pleats expand, making lots of room for the food and water the whale takes in.

This photo shows the snouts of humpbacks feeding in Alaska. GREGORY KAUFMAN, PACIFIC WHALE FOUNDATION

3

Toothed Whales

A TREMENDOUS VARIETY OF CETACEANS IS INCLUDED among the toothed whales. Along with the larger species, which are called whales because of their size, there are the smaller dolphins and porpoises. These are generally better known than the whales, both because they are more numerous and because their smaller size makes them easier to keep in captivity.

Odontocetes have a rounded, fatty deposit on the forehead called the melon, which is more pronounced in some than in others. One completely unique trait of toothed whales is

The beluga has a very prominent melon on its forehead.
SEA WORLD PHOTO

49

their single nostril, or blowhole. All other mammals have two openings from the outside into the nasal cavities. Inside the skull of a toothed whale, the nasal passages separate into right and left halves, as in other mammals.

The name "toothed whales" can be misleading, for some of these animals have no functional teeth at all. But all of them show teeth in one or both jaws, even if they never break through to the outside. When there are many teeth, as in killer whales, they all look similar. Among some whales, only the males have teeth. Males of the mysterious beaked whales have only two teeth at the tip of the lower jaw. These teeth take on very strange shapes in some beaked whales and are probably used in battles between the males for mates. In almost all male narwhals, just the left front tooth develops. It becomes a long, straight tusk that sticks out in front of the animal.

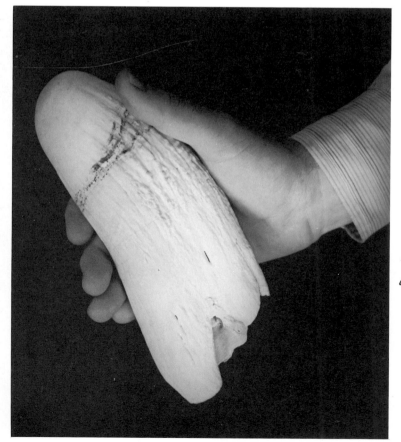

This giant tooth is from a sperm whale. NOAA

*You can see the many strong, pointed teeth of the
killer whale in this photo.* SEA WORLD PHOTO

Sperm Whales

The strange profile of the sperm whale is quite familiar. These unusual animals have a huge square head that can occupy 40 percent of the length of the animal in males. The name "sperm whale" comes from the fine oil, called spermaceti, which fills much of the gigantic head. This valuable product made the sperm whale a special prize for whalers. Also in the head is the largest brain of any animal, protected by the largest skull of any mammal.

About two-thirds of the way down the sperm whale's body is a hump on the back, followed by a row of smaller bumps. The skin of sperm whales often looks wrinkled and is brownish-black in color. Sometimes there are lighter markings on the underside of the body. The lower jaw is narrow and contains from eighteen to twenty-five teeth. When the mouth is closed, the teeth fit neatly into sockets in the upper jaw.

The strange head of the sperm whale is actually a gigantic nose. In other whales the blowhole is on top of the head. But the sperm whale's blowhole is way out at the tip of the nose, on the left side, and the nasal passages extend all the way from behind the mouth to the tip of the snout. The valuable spermaceti oil is contained within the spermaceti organ, which is covered by a thick, muscular membrane. Below the spermaceti organ is a region of spongy cells also full of oil, called "junk" by whalers. The left nasal passage connects directly with the blowhole. The right passage is much smaller in diameter than the left and links two different air sacs, one at the front of the head and the other at the back. The complex arrangement of oil, air sacs, and nasal passages is almost certainly important to the sperm whale for suc-

The sperm whale has an enormous head and a narrow lower jaw. D. E. GASKIN

cessful diving and for communication, but we don't understand just what all the different parts do.

Sperm whales are very vocal, making low, moaning creaks as well as high-pitched clicks. The sounds can be heard for miles, even by humans, whose ears are not adapted to hearing in water. Some of the sperm whale's sounds are probably used to communicate with other sperm whales through the dark depths of the ocean. But different sounds are most likely used in echolocation, to find food.

Sperm whales dive to great depths; one animal was tracked to almost 10,000 feet (3,048 meters). The pressure at such depths is enormous, but the whales are well adapted to it. Sperm whales can remain submerged for an hour or more. When they surface, they let out a dramatic blow, then lie at the surface taking smaller breaths before diving again.

All sorts of strange things, including a boot and a glass fishing float, have been found in sperm whale stomachs. But their chief food is squid of many different kinds, including the giant squid, which inhabits the depths of the ocean. Giant squid may reach 60 feet (18.2 meters) in length, measured from the tips of the long tentacles to the end of the body. This measurement is somewhat misleading since much of this length is just tentacle. Rarely do sperm whales come to the surface of the sea while battling with giant squid; we mostly know about these fights by observing the round scars made on the whales' bodies by the squid's suckers. But, judging from the success of sperm whales in feeding on squid, such battles must be rare. Some scientists believe that sperm whales can emit a sonar wave that stuns or kills its prey. This method would explain how an animal with no weapons other than its teeth could successfully attack and eat such well-armed animals as squid. Now and then, the sperm whale intestine contains a strange waxy substance called ambergris, which may be formed around the remains of squid beaks. Ambergris has been especially valued as an ingredient for perfume, since it helps hold the scent, although it is illegal to use ambergris for perfumes in the United States today. Synthetic substitutes for ambergris are now available.

Sperm whales often live in groups of fifty or more individuals. The older males spend most of the year alone or with a few companions, but females and young sperm whales usually stay together. Sperm whales tend to migrate toward the poles in the spring and return to milder climates during the fall. The lone males travel much farther poleward than the females and young.

The sperm whale has two close relatives, the dwarf and pygmy sperm whales. The dwarf sperm whale is no longer than 8 feet (2.4 meters), and the pygmy sperm whale reaches about 11 feet (3.4 meters). Not much is known about these two animals.

Arctic Ice Dwellers

The narwhal and the beluga, or white whale, are two related whales that normally stay close to the Arctic ice. Both are small, the narwhal reaching 16 feet (5 meters) and the beluga just under 15 feet (4.6 meters), and both have been extensively hunted by natives and commercial hunters. Belugas and narwhals lack a dorsal fin. They have thick skin and a thick blubber layer, which help protect them from the Arctic cold.

The narwhal is a peculiar whale. The long, single tusk of the male, which sticks out from the left side of its jaw, can be up to 8½ feet long (2.6 meters). The tusk is quite easily

A carving of a male narwhal. NATIONAL MUSEUM OF MAN, NATIONAL MUSEUMS OF CANADA, NEG. # 78-1907

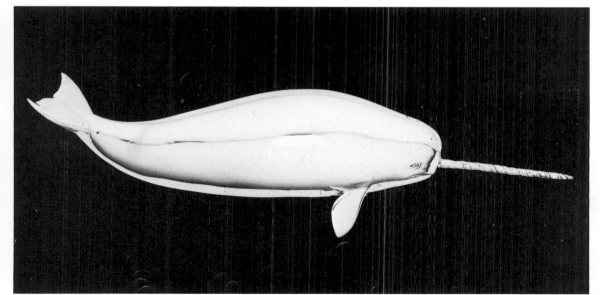

broken, and many adult males have tusks with broken tips. The tip is always polished, as if it has been rubbing against something, even when it is broken. There are many theories about the uses of the tusk, but since it is normally found only in adult males, it probably functions somehow in reproductive behavior. Males have scars on their heads more often than females, but the scars are not the deep puncture wounds one would expect if the tusks were used in energetic battle. Male narwhals are sometimes seen crossing tusks with one another, both above and below the surface of the water. Some scientists think that a male narwhal can somehow compare the length of his tusk with that of other males, and that those with longer tusks win out over the other males. But there are also researchers who believe the tusk may help carry sounds by which the males communicate with one another or with the females.

Narwhals may travel in large numbers, even thousands at one time. These large groups actually consist of many smaller ones of no more than twenty animals. Females with young may stay together, as do adult males. Sometimes a group will consist of both males and females. Narwhals stay in deeper water close to the ice, feeding on fish, shrimp, and squid.

Narwhals are hunted for the "ivory" of their tusks and for their meat, blubber, and skin, which are valued by native hunters. Despite hunting, the narwhal is still abundant in certain areas, since its habit of staying close to the sea ice sometimes makes it difficult for people to get near it.

Unlike the adult narwhal, the adult beluga is completely white, while newborns are pinkish brown or gray. They remain gray until they are adults. Belugas have irregular teeth—eight to eleven in each upper jaw, eight or nine on

A beluga. NEW YORK ZOOLOGICAL SOCIETY PHOTO

each lower jaw—which they use to feed on fish, shrimp, and octopus. Belugas sometimes travel up rivers during the summer, making them easy prey for hunters. They often live in large groups and are very vocal, making a great variety of chirps and whistles, which can occasionally even be heard in the air.

In some areas, belugas are quite abundant, but in others only a few remain. They are still hunted by natives, who harvest them for leather made from their skin, meat, and blubber.

KILLER WHALES

The killer whale is a feared hunter in the sea, attacking seals, other whales, walruses, penguins, sea turtles, and just about anything else it can get its teeth into. Killers need to eat lots of food. Shamu, a captive killer whale at Sea World in Ohio, eats as much as 125 pounds (55 kilograms) of fish in one day.

When captured and tamed, the killer whale can be a gentle, friendly creature. Perhaps one reason killer whales can become so tame and well trained is that they live in social groups in the wild. This social behavior leads to a need for companionship and a willingness to cooperate with others. Up to thirty live and hunt together, cooperating in bringing down their prey. These groups are called pods. A large pod may even attack an adult blue whale, tearing at it from all sides. When killer whales are nearby, seals will jump out of the water and onto the ice for protection. But that doesn't

Killer whales in captivity can be very friendly to humans. MARINE WORLD/AFRICA USA

Trained killer whales Shamu and Namu perform at Sea World in Cleveland, Ohio.
SEA WORLD/CLEVELAND, OHIO

Tame killer whales will even let humans ride on them.
SEA WORLD/CLEVELAND, OHIO

A pod of killer whales. The tall fins belong to males, while the short ones are on the females. © PETER THOMAS

necessarily save them. One scientist observed a pod that discovered a seal floating along on a chunk of ice. The whales circled around it, spy-hopping to look at it, for about five minutes. Then they swam away, turned, and approached the seal again as a group. As they neared it, they surfaced twice, close to the seal's refuge, making a big wave with their powerful flukes in the otherwise calm water. When the wave reached the floating ice, tipping it over, the seal was dumped into the water. The whales immediately rushed toward the spot. Although the scientist didn't see the whales eating the seal, it was clear that their behavior was aimed at catching the seal for food.

Killer whales have a striking color pattern. They are shiny black, except for white patches just above and behind each eye and a white area on the underside that extends over the lower jaw, down the belly, and up along the sides. The white continues all the way to the flukes, which are white underneath. There is also a gray marking across the back behind the dorsal fin. The exact area of these markings differs from one population of killers to another, and the gray patch appears to be different from one individual to the next.

The female's dorsal fin is similar to that of a dolphin's; the fin of the adult male is very large and triangular. Killer whales can easily be identified by this distinctive fin, which may be 6 feet (1.8 meters) tall in a full-grown male. The male can be over 30 feet (9.2 meters) long, while the female reaches 21 feet (7 meters).

Killer whales can be seen in all the oceans of the world, from the Arctic and Antarctic to the warm seas near the equator. They have been killed by commercial whalers, but not to the same extent as the other great whales.

The killer whale in front is a male; the one behind is a female. It is easy to tell them apart by the size and shape of their dorsal fins.
© PETER THOMAS

61

A captive pilot whale. SEA WORLD PHOTO

SOME SMALL WHALES

There are several small species of whales. The two kinds of
pilot whales are dark gray to black, with gray markings on
their bellies. They have blunt noses, and teeth in both the
upper and lower jaws. The long-finned pilot whale, which
has long, graceful flippers, can reach 20 feet (6 meters) in
length, but the short-finned pilot whale is slightly smaller.
Pilot whales live in large groups, sometimes several hundred
at a time, and may travel with bottlenose dolphins. This
habit of group living has made long-finned pilot whales sub-
ject to hunting. In the Faeroe Islands, pilot whales are
sighted offshore, then driven into shallow water, where they
are killed. These whales have been hunted this way for hundreds of years. No more than a thousand animals are taken in
one year, however, so the population of pilot whales there is
not depleted by hunting. In Newfoundland, however, such
hunts in the recent past may well have affected pilot whale
populations.

The pygmy killer whale is a rare whale of tropical waters that reaches only about 8 feet (2.4 meters) in length. These animals have rounded heads and are dark gray with white markings underneath.

The false killer whale is larger than the pygmy, as long as 20 feet (6 meters). It is almost completely black in color and lives widely in warm and tropical waters. Like pilot whales, false killer whales live in large groups, often along with other cetaceans such as bottlenose dolphins.

The melon-headed whales look similar to false killer whales, but their snouts are more pointed, and they are smaller, getting no longer than 9 feet (2.7 meters). They are black with light markings on their bellies. Like the other small whales, melon-headed whales live in large groups, often associated with dolphins, and are widely distributed in the tropics.

False killer whales out at sea.
R. L. PITMAN/REPRINTED FROM LEATHERWOOD, ET AL. 1982

The Mysterious Beaked Whales

Modern science has given us knowledge of many of nature's mysteries. But there are still more puzzles to be solved, more unknown facts to be discovered. The beaked whales provide plenty of questions for the curious. Although these creatures are among the largest whales—the biggest found so far was 42 feet (12.8 meters) long—we know almost nothing about them. There are about eighteen species of beaked whales. Generally, they have streamlined bodies with wide flukes and small flippers. Their jaws are elongated into a pointed snout, and some beaked whales have a bulging forehead so that they look a bit like giant porpoises.

You can see that the dorsal fin is set far back on this Baird's beaked whale. Notice the scars on its back. These are probably made by the paired teeth of other males in fights.
K. C. BALCOMB/REPRINTED FROM LEATHERWOOD, ET AL. 1982

Most beaked whales are known only because their bones have been found washed up on beaches. One kind has a mouthful of teeth; the other species have only a few teeth. Many species are completely toothless, except for a pair in the lower jaw of the male. The shapes of these can be very strange. One beaked whale is called the ginkgo-toothed whale because the male's two teeth are rounded like the ginkgo tree's fan-shaped leaves. Males of another kind have unique teeth that grow outside the lower jaw and backward, then curve over the upper jaw so that the animal can barely open its mouth. Male beaked whales often show pairs of scars on their bodies that appear to be from the teeth of other males. No one, however, has ever seen two beaked whales fighting.

It is hard to know whether beaked whales are very rare or if they just live in the open ocean far from shore, where humans seldom go. At least one species, the goosebeak whale, lives in almost every ocean. Others are so scarce, or so secretive, that only rarely are bones even found. Most beaked whales probably feed on squid and deep-sea fishes.

4

Whale Mysteries

SCIENTIFIC RESEARCH ON WHALES IS QUITE NEW AND IS DIF-
ficult to carry out. Giant whales cannot be kept in captivity,
and experiments can't be easily done with them. We know a
lot more about the smaller cetaceans, simply because they
can be confined and studied much more easily. There are several mysteries about whales, some of which we may never
solve. But scientists are hard at work trying to understand
the giants of the sea that share our world.

CETACEAN SONAR

Although scientists have studied sound production and the
reception of the returning sonar signals in porpoises and dolphins, many questions remain to be answered, even for those
small odontocetes. We do not know just how the sounds are
created, since, as mentioned in Chapter 1, cetaceans lack a
voice box such as ours. Some process involving the complex
systems of air passages in the head is almost certainly involved. The fatty odontocete melon appears to function in
focusing the sound. The melon is made up of a variety of fats,
with differing qualities, so that its structure could affect the
way sound waves leave the head.

Just how odontocetes receive the returning echoes is also unclear. Some scientists believe that the ear is isolated from the rest of the skull by the foamy tissues that surround it. Others believe that the jawbones or the fatty tissue in the jaws carries sound waves to the ears.

Chances are that all or almost all odontocetes use sonar to some extent to find their way and locate food, but we know little about the actual sonar abilities of most large ones. We do know that many odontocete whales are very vocal—the beluga has been called the sea canary, it is so noisy. The various whales that live in pods are also vocal. Some of their sounds are probably involved in echolocation and others in communication—we just don't know. Also, it has been assumed that baleen whales do not use sonar, but again, we do not know enough to say for sure. Many baleen whales produce a great variety of sounds, and some of them may be involved in finding food rather than in communicating.

THE SOCIAL LIFE OF WHALES

Whales vary greatly in their social behavior. Some, such as killer and pilot whales, live in closely knit pods that hunt cooperatively. Others, like gray whales and humpbacks, gather together for birthing and early care of their young but live independently during nonbreeding seasons. We are still just learning about how these whales interact during the times they are found together. For example, we still don't know the social role of the humpback's eerie songs, even though they have been studied in great detail. As already discussed, only the males sing, and only while the animals are in warm seas caring for the young. The latest suggestion is that the singing lets other males know something about how big and strong or how experienced the singer is, much as the ant-

Although killer whales have been kept in captivity, we still know very little about their social interactions in the wild.
© PETER THOMAS

lers of male elk and the horns on mountain sheep rams do.

Many whales are so difficult to observe that we have few facts to help us understand their social relationships. We know almost nothing about how beaked whales live, for instance. And our knowledge of the lives even of common whales is very limited. For example, what are the relationships among the members of a killer whale pod? Is there a leader? Are the animals related to one another? The life of whales in the sea is so different from that of mammals on land that it is especially difficult to unravel the mysteries of whale social behavior. But, because of the great interest in whales these days, we are learning more and more all the time.

BREACHING

A whale sometimes leaps straight up out of the water, propelling its gigantic body high in the air above the sea, and crashes down on its side or back with a huge splash. Right, humpback, gray, and sperm whales are particularly known to perform this impressive feat, called breaching. Why do whales breach, an act that must take a great deal of effort and energy? We don't know, but several reasons have been suggested. Some scientists believe breaching communicates a message to whales nearby, while others think that perhaps the animals are trying to loosen the parasites that cling to their bodies. Whatever its function, breaching is an amazing display of cetacean strength—lifting so many tons of flesh completely out of the water must take enormous power.

A humpback breaches.
J. MICHAEL WILLIAMSON/EARTH VIEWS

STRANDING

For unknown reasons, whales occasionally swim into shallow water and become stranded. This tendency spelled great fortune for prehistoric humans, who were suddenly presented with an abundant source of meat and raw materials. But today, stranding seems a tragic waste, especially since so many whale species have been drastically reduced in numbers. Usually, an individual animal is stranded, tossed onto the beach by the waves and left high and dry at low tide. But sometimes, a whole pod of whales, usually smaller species such as false killers or pilot whales, will swim into shallow water and be left behind when the tide goes out. The strangest thing about strandings is that when people try to rescue the animals and set them afloat again, the whales usually stubbornly return to the beach.

Several possible causes of stranding have been proposed. Some scientists think the gentle slope of a beach is confusing to the whale's sonar, as more than 80 percent of mass strandings occur in such areas. Other suggested causes are parasitic infections of the ear, which interfere with interpreting the sonar system; unusual weather conditions; attack by

Concerned people try to help this stranded gray whale by splashing it to keep its skin wet.
DOUGLAS MACPHAIL, C/O PETER THOMAS

Stranded whales usually die, like this beached baby humpback.
GREGORY KAUFMAN,
PACIFIC WHALE FOUNDATION

predators; and confusing underwater sounds.

Chances are that there is more than one cause for stranding. It may be, for an individual whale, anyway, a last desperate attempt to survive. Whales must come up to breathe, and a very sick and weak whale might have great difficulty swimming up or staying near the surface. By coming into shallow water, the whale can keep its blowhole out of the water and breathe without exerting any effort.

Mass strandings, however, are especially hard to explain. Why would a whole pod of whales risk death in this way? It is hard to imagine that all of them could be that badly infested with parasites or that all were sick at the same time. By looking at one typical mass stranding of false killer whales, perhaps we can get some idea of what might be happening when whales behave this way. In July 1976, a pod of thirty false killer whales swam into the shallow water on an island off the Florida coast. Fortunately, scientists were alerted to the stranding and came to investigate. They found that one large male whale at the front of the pod was bleeding from his right ear. This male eventually died, and the scientists discovered that his ear was badly infested by parasites. A few of the other whales had cuts in their skin but otherwise seemed healthy. The whales were constantly making noises: squeals, squawks, chirps, and squeaks could be heard, even far out of the water. Different individuals seemed to be making different sounds. When people waded into the water and tried to turn the whales seaward, the animals refused to leave. The people did what they could to help the whales—spreading suntan lotion over their backs, which were out of the water, and splashing water over them so they wouldn't dry out. After three days, the big male finally died. The tight formation of the rest of the pod then loosened up, and when people herded them back toward the sea, the animals left.

We can't be sure just what happened in this case, but we can make some intelligent guesses. The large male was clearly weak and sick; he had a hard time staying upright, even in the shallow water. Maybe he was the leader of the pod, and the rest of the animals stayed with him because he led them into the shallows. Or it may be that false killer whales, which frequently become stranded, have such strong social ties that they often or always accompany a weakened member of the pod when it enters shallow water. We simply don't know enough about the relationships of these animals to give an answer.

These lower jaws were taken from a group of at least forty-one sperm whales which were stranded on an Oregon beach.
GREENPEACE FOUNDATION

5

People and Whales

EVER SINCE THE FIRST WHALE WAS BEACHED NEAR A human settlement, people have been fascinated by the strangeness and gigantic size of whales. Prehistoric people must have stood in awe of the great rows of huge baleen plates, unlike anything known in land animals. They must have wondered where these enormous animals came from and how they lived. They also must have been grateful for the sudden and mysterious presence of so much meat, oil, and other useful raw materials.

This male killer whale is acting as if he is curious about the nearby boat and the people on it. © OLIVER THOMAS

While some early humans took advantage of whales only when they were beached, others put out to sea to find them. For thousands of years, whales have been hunted along the coastlines of Norway, Spain, Japan, and North America. A typical method of hunting involved wounding a whale with a harpoon, marking it, then returning to shore to wait while the animal died a slow death. If the whale sank instead of floated, it was lost. Although this kind of hunting resulted in an agonizing death for the whale and in the waste of many animals, it did not endanger the survival of any whale species. Relatively few whales could be hunted by these primitive methods, so people could hunt whales without reducing their populations. Only along the coast of Spain, where the Basque people hunted right whales, were whale numbers seriously affected by early whaling. By the fourteenth century, Basque whalers were already journeying over a day's distance from shore, because they had so depleted the whales that lived nearer.

Starting in the sixteenth century, whale hunting began to change. Up until then, whaling had been carried out only to provide needed meat and raw materials. But then rich merchants of northern Europe began to see whaling as a way of making money. Whale oil, extracted from the abundant blubber, was a valuable product used for lubrication, for making soap, and as fuel for lighting. At that time, there was no electricity, and a clean-burning oil like that from whales was highly prized. Spermaceti oil was especially valuable as fuel for smokeless candles. Baleen was used for many purposes. In those days before plastic, baleen provided a strong, flexible material for corset stays, clock springs, shoehorns, fishing gear, and other products. Many European countries sent whaling ships to the Arctic during the summer. By the seventeenth century, "blubber towns," that existed for the sole purpose of processing captured whales, were built all along the coasts of the small islands off East Greenland, such as Spitzbergen.

Whaling was very profitable. The baleen and oil from just one right whale brought twice as much money as it took to outfit a whaling ship. Therefore, if each ship took only one whale, it made a handsome profit. In the eighteenth century, America became a whaling center, with several important ports along the New England coast. During the first half of the nineteenth century, the United States was the biggest whaling nation in the world, with four times as many whaling men than all the other countries put together. American whaling in this era was the inspiration for Herman Melville's great novel, *Moby Dick*, about a magnificent sperm whale and the men who tried to catch him.

A Hazardous Occupation

Whaling in those days was a dangerous job. The trip to the whaling grounds was sometimes long and dull. As sailing ships, the early whaling vessels had to rely on the winds to get them where they were going. Once there, the search began. A sailor climbed one of the ship's masts. He stood on a small platform called the crow's nest, with a single barrel hoop to keep him from falling down. When he spotted the blow of a whale, he cried out, "Thar she blows!" The hunt was on. Small catcher boats, only about 30 feet (9.2 meters) long, were put over the side. A harpooner stood in the bow of the catcher. The harpoon was attached to a long, coiled rope that was tied to a post near the rear of the boat. When the catcher got close enough, the harpoon was thrown. Then the wounded whale tried to get away. The slack in the rope was

This scratchboard drawing shows how dangerous whaling was in the early days.
LEONARD EVERETT FISHER

taken up, and the catcher was pulled along by the whale as it desperately tried to escape. This was a very dangerous time for the men in the catcher, since they were completely helpless. Many catchers were overturned, dumping the crew into the water, and some were dragged underwater by diving whales. But if all went according to plan, the whale wore itself out, and more and more harpoons were thrown until the animal finally died. Then it was towed by the catcher back to the bigger ship for processing.

These early whalers didn't think about the future of the whales. They just hunted and killed as many as they could, especially sperm and right whales. By the middle of the nineteenth century, the stocks of different kinds of whales in the Atlantic were very small. When the animals became scarce in one area, the whalers simply traveled farther to make their catch, until they depleted whales there. Then they moved on again. When the transcontinental railroad was completed in 1869, a link of West to East was established. Then the products from whales killed along the West Coast could easily be transported to the more populated East. It wasn't long before the abundant gray whale, which migrated so conveniently up and down the coast, became scarce.

MORE EFFICIENT KILLING

Up until the late 1800s, only the slow-swimming whales were hunted. The speedy rorquals could easily outdistance the fastest catcher boats, so they were left alone. But, unfortunately for whales, modern technology improved the speed and efficiency of the whaling industry. Norway had been a major whaling nation for a long time, and a Norwegian named Svend Foyn revolutionized whaling during the 1860s. He invented a motorized catcher boat, 94 feet (29 meters) long, that was equipped with a deadly cannon-fired, exploding harpoon. This new catcher boat could easily track down rorquals. To process all the whales caught by these more effective means, shore stations were built where the blubber was rendered into oil and the meat and bone were ground up into fertilizer.

These men are just beginning to remove the blubber from a humpback. NFB PHOTOTEQUE/PHOTO BY C. LUND, 1948

You can see the layer of blubber which the man is expertly removing with his special tool, called a flensing knife. NOAA (1951)

The new, deadly whaling methods quickly depleted rorqual stocks, first near Norway, then farther and farther away as the whalers moved with their prey. Other countries joined the force of mechanized whalers, killing more and more whales. The United States, however, was slow to give up sail-powered whaling ships, and whaling in this country declined.

Whaling for profit was a wasteful industry. When whales were abundant, their carcasses were often set adrift after only partial processing. The meat, which is a high-protein food valued by the Inuit and the Japanese, was turned into cheap fertilizer and later into animal feed, if it was used at all.

Modern techniques kept the whaling industry going, despite the ever-decreasing numbers of whales. Large ships, called factory ships, were built so that whales could be processed out at sea. The whalers then could follow the smaller numbers of whales more easily. Deadlier harpoons and better catchers also came into use.

This dead minke whale lies on the deck of a factory ship. JAPAN WHALING ASSOCIATION

Saving the Whales

Conservation efforts for whales began in the 1930s, but for a long time they were ineffective. In 1946 the International Whaling Commission (IWC) was set up to regulate whaling. Many nations signed the agreement establishing the commission, including major whaling nations such as the U.S.S.R. and Norway. Although the IWC was established to save whales from extinction, it also existed to help the whaling industry. It was difficult to meet both these goals at the same time, so for many years the IWC merely slowed the disappearance of whales. More and more species became increasingly rare.

The IWC meets every year to establish "safe" quotas of each great whale species for each member nation. The numbers of whales that may be killed are supposed to be based on estimates of how many whales there are. Since it is very difficult to count whales accurately, the lack of good population estimates was often used as an excuse to allow too many whales to be harvested.

The decline in whale populations went on until the 1970s with little sign of hope. Then, in 1972, the United States Congress passed the Marine Mammal Protection Act, which forbade the killing of marine mammals of any kind in U.S. waters, the only exception being subsistence hunting by native peoples such as the Alaskan Inuit. Since that time, international interest in saving whales from extinction has increased every year. The IWC has moved slowly toward protecting whales. In 1979 factory ships were outlawed, except for use with minke whales in some Antarctic waters. The biggest blow to commercial whaling, however, came in 1983, when the IWC voted a complete moratorium, or suspension, on commercial whaling to begin in late 1985. But, unfortunately, this vote may not end commercial whaling. Japan, Norway, and the U.S.S.R., which are the biggest whaling nations, have all refused to go along with the moratorium. They plan to continue after 1985. These nations say that whaling is a vital activity for some of their citizens and that its end will spell economic ruin for those people. The Japanese argue that whale meat is important to them as food, and are eager to point out that no part of a harvested whale is wasted. Japan, Norway, and the U.S.S.R. hope they can get the IWC to allow them to carry out some coastal whaling in the same way the native peoples of Alaska and Greenland are allowed to harvest some whales that they claim are necessary to their economy.

When whaling began, there were no substitutes for the fine spermaceti oil of the sperm whale or the flexible baleen of baleen whales. The abundant whale oil was the major source of fuel for artificial lighting until the mid-1800s, and whale meat was highly valued by native peoples and the Japanese. While all whale products have substitutes today, the

This once magnificent humpback, bagged by Alaskan whalers in 1938, was turned into a variety of products derived from its oil, baleen, and meat. NOAA (1938)

different parts of the whale are still put to many uses. The meat is eaten, and the oil is used in making soap, shortening, cosmetics, lubricants for delicate machinery, and other products. Baleen is still used for fishing poles and shoehorns, and the bones and intestines are processed into fertilizer. Hormones are extracted from the glands, and sperm whale junk is made into gelatin, glue, and photographic film.

Today, only the sperm whale still exists in about the same numbers as it once did. The blue, sei, fin, right, bowhead, and humpback whales are all endangered. The population of gray whales along the Pacific coast of North America has recovered, but elsewhere these animals are extinct or almost so. Minke whales are quite abundant, partly because there are so few blue whales left to compete with them for krill. Little is known about the actual population of the Bryde's whale, although it seems to be much less abundant than before.

While the whaling nations argue that some whale species are not diminishing and will not become extinct even with continued whaling, conservationists believe that without a ban on commercial whaling, whales will disappear from the Earth. Unfortunately, all nations that kill whales do not belong to the IWC. So even if Norway, Japan, and the U.S.S.R. decide to abide by the IWC moratorium, some whaling may continue. We can only hope that it is not enough to further endanger these magnificent animals.

WHALES AND HUMANS TOGETHER

Since ancient times, a bond has existed between cetaceans and humans. Ancient Greek stories tell of boys and dolphins that were friends, and now and then a story about a dolphin saving a drowning human is told today. But the larger cetaceans seem to have a mysterious relationship to humans, too, despite the cruelty people have inflicted upon them through whaling. When scientists dive into the water to study whales, the whales are often just as curious as the humans and actively avoid harming them. Dr. Gregory Kaufman of the Pacific Whale Foundation writes of an encounter with a baby humpback whale, its mother, and their escort, which in many ways is typical. As Dr. Kaufman approached the whales underwater, the baby spied him and swam in his direction. It came to within a few yards of him and stopped. Then the calf somersaulted, turned, rolled over on its back, and swam by upside down. It was acting as if it wanted a playmate. As Dr. Kaufman surfaced for air, the calf joined him. Then it began to swim very close, and its powerful flipper was about to hit the scientist. But just in time, the calf turned and avoided swatting him. Next the mother came along. Mammal mothers are generally very protective of their youngsters. A person who gets between a moose or grizzly bear and her baby

Coastal peoples around the world have respected and honored whales in many ways. Here their images are used as part of the entrance to a Northwest coastal Kwakiutl Indian graveyard in British Columbia, Canada. © PETER THOMAS

is in great danger. But the mother whale was just as careful with the scientist as her baby. She could easily have battered him with her flukes as she swam by. But instead, she glided safely past him before again beating her tail.

Stories like this are very common. A group of scientists encountered a pod of rare pygmy killer whales at sea. They didn't know what the animals were, but slipped over the side to join and photograph them. The whales had almost certainly never seen people before; they were completely wild. Yet, after being briefly touched by one scientist, one of the whales swam back to him for another pat! Wild gray whales in Mexican lagoons, especially babies, sometimes approach the boats carrying curious whale-watchers and come right alongside to be stroked. They may swim up to a boat, turn sideways in the water to look at the people, and gently rock the boat. We know that whales are social animals among themselves, but no one can explain their apparent friendliness to humans. Because they are wild, however, these giant animals should not be completely trusted. Most human encounters with gray whales are friendly or neutral, but now and then someone is killed by a whale.

Whales captured for research and entertainment purposes can become very fond of their human friends. Porpoises, dolphins, and the smaller whales that can be kept in captivity learn tricks easily. They recognize their keepers and enjoy their company in the water. They will even stick their heads out of the water to be stroked.

Cetaceans are unique, intelligent, and fascinating animals. We humans can learn a great deal by getting to know them better. Let us hope that we make the kind of decisions that will allow these special creatures to continue to share our world with us.

A zoo keeper feeds his cetacean friend, killer whale Moby Doll, at the Stanley Park Zoo in Vancouver, B.C. NFB PHOTOTEQUE/ GAR LUNNEY, 1964

Scientific and Common Names of Whales

BALEEN WHALES—*MYSTICETI*

FAMILY *BALAENIDAE:* THE RIGHT WHALES

Bowhead or Greenland right whale	*Balaena mysticetus*
Black right whale, right whale or northern right whale	*Eubalaena glacialis*
Black right whale, right whale or southern right whale	*Eubalaena australis*
Pygmy right whale	*Caperea marginata*

FAMILY *BALAENOPTERIDAE:* THE RORQUALS AND HUMPBACK

Blue whale	*Balaenoptera musculus*
Fin whale	*Balaenoptera physalus*
Sei whale	*Balaenoptera borealis*
Bryde's whale	*Balaenoptera edeni*
Minke whale or piked whale	*Balaenoptera acutorostrata*
Humpback whale	*Megaptera novaeangliae*

FAMILY *ESCHRICHTIIDAE:* THE GRAY WHALE

Gray whale	*Eschrichtius robustus*

TOOTHED WHALES—*ODONTOCETI*
(Only whales discussed in this book are listed.)

FAMILY *ZIPHIIDAE:* THE BEAKED WHALES

About 18 species, in genera *Mesoplodon, Ziphius, Tasmacetus, Berardius,* and *Hyperoodon*

FAMILY *PHYSETERIDAE:* THE SPERM WHALES

Sperm whale	*Physeter macrocephalus*
Pygmy sperm whale	*Kogia breviceps*
Dwarf sperm whale	*Kogia simus*

FAMILY *MONODONTIDAE:* THE NARWHAL AND BELUGA

Narwhal	*Monodon monoceros*
Beluga or white whale	*Delphinapterus leucas*

FAMILY *DELHPINIDAE:* THE OCEANIC DOLPHINS AND SOME WHALES

Killer whale	*Orcinus orca*
Pilot whale, Long-Finned pilot whale, blackfish	*Globicephala melaena*
Short-Finned pilot whale, blackfish	*Globicephala macrorhynchus*
Pygmy killer whale	*Feresa attenuata*
False killer whale	*Pseudorca crassidens*
Melon-Headed whale	*Peponocephala electra*

Index